VIKINGS

BY

SUSAN HARRISON

EXPLORING BRITISH
HISTORY

©2017

Book Life
King's Lynn
Norfolk PE30 4LS

ISBN: 978-1-78637-075-4

All rights reserved
Printed in Malaysia

A catalogue record for this book
is available from the British Library.

Written by:
Susan Harrison

Edited by:
Grace Jones

Designed by:
Natalie Carr

PHOTO CREDITS

VIKINGS

CONTENTS

Words that look like *this* are explained in the glossary on page 30.

WHO WERE THE VIKINGS?

The Vikings came from Scandinavia, which are the countries that we now call Denmark, Sweden and Norway. They were great warriors and were feared throughout Europe. They sailed across the North Sea and the northern Atlantic Ocean in order to *invade* countries, create *settlements*, farm and trade.

NORWAY

SWED

DENMARK

ENGLAND

THE VIKINGS SETTLED IN MANY DIFFERENT PLACES IN BRITAIN.

■ VIKING SETTLEMENTS

■ VIKING HOMELAND

In AD 793 the Vikings attacked a monastery at Lindisfarne, which is a small island off the north-east coast of England. This attack marked the beginning of the *Viking Age*. As well as being fierce warriors, the Vikings were hard-working people who built new farms, villages, forts and towns.

They were also skilled sailors, *merchants*, *craftworkers* and *explorers*. Many places across Europe today have Viking names, and Viking words are still used in some languages, including English.

VIKINGS WERE GREATLY FEARED AND OFTEN BURNED DOWN WHOLE VILLAGES WHEN THEY INVADED.

Archaeologists have found many different *artefacts* that help us to understand how the Vikings lived their way of life, and their beliefs. Many of these have been found in Viking burial mounds.

The Vikings were also merchants and traded their goods with different countries. Craftsmen made combs, knives, jewellery, pottery and leather goods to sell. In Turkey, they traded their wares in the colourful markets of the capital of *Constantinople* alongside spices, silks and jewellery from Asia.

At first, the Vikings would attack other countries for plunder and did not settle. They began to invade other countries when it became difficult to find suitable farmland on their own land.

The Vikings were famous for their shipbuilding. These skills played a vital role in their ability to invade other countries from the sea. Over time, they invaded parts of many other countries, including America, Canada and Russia.

INVADERS AND SETTLERS

During the beginning of the Viking Age, Vikings would cross the seas from Scandinavia to invade defenceless villages on the British coastline looking for gold, silver and *livestock*. They had a fearsome reputation for killing or capturing anyone who stood in their way before heading home with their stolen goods.

The most frightening Viking warriors were called 'berserkers'. They were chosen for their fighting skills and would sometimes take drugs to help work themselves up into a terrifying rage before they attacked.

Viking raiders were fierce and strong and spread fear all over Britain. Some of them were full-time warriors, but some were farmers who left for raids in the spring after their crops were planted and returned to their farms in the autumn for the harvest.

THIS VIKING SWORD IS KEPT IN THE VIKING MUSEUM IN HEDEBY IN GERMANY AND IT IS A GOOD EXAMPLE OF THE WEAPONS THAT THE VIKINGS USED WHEN THEY ATTACKED.

Viking kings grew rich from their raids and were able to supply and train large armies. As farmland in their own countries became scarce, they turned their attention to settling in the places they attacked.

From AD 865, the Vikings used their large armies to invade Britain and in AD 866 they invaded Northumbria and the city of York. In the next few years, they conquered most of Britain and set up settlements across the country.

THE CITY OF JORVIK (YORK) WAS ONE OF THE FIRST PLACES IN BRITAIN TO BE INVADED BY THE VIKINGS. AT THE TIME, YORK WAS IN NORTHUMBRIA. IT IS NOW A LARGE CITY IN YORKSHIRE.

THE CITY OF JORVIK (YORK) WAS ONE OF THE FIRST PLACES IN BRITAIN TO BE INVADED BY THE VIKINGS. AT THE TIME, YORK WAS IN NORTHUMBRIA. IT IS NOW A LARGE CITY IN YORKSHIRE.

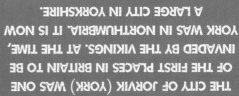

Over time, women and children arrived with the invaders and the Vikings started to build houses in the lands that the warriors had won. They settled all over Britain and built many new towns, such as Derby, which is now a modern-day city.

THIS IS A MODEL OF A VIKING SETTLEMENT. THE INVADERS WORKED HARD TO BUILD THEIR VILLAGES AND TOWNS SO THAT THEIR FAMILIES COULD LIVE AND WORK IN THEM.

THE VIKINGS WERE FEARSOME WARRIORS AND THEIR ARMOUR INCLUDED HELMETS, WHICH HELPED TO PROTECT THEIR HEADS AND FACES AND MADE THEM LOOK FRIGHTENING TO THEIR ENEMIES.

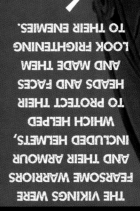

After successfully invading most of the country, the Vikings attacked Wessex in January AD 871. During the Battle of Ashdown, they met their match and were defeated by the Saxon King Ethelred and his brother Alfred.

AN IMAGE OF KING ETHELRED AT THE BATTLE OF ASHDOWN, WHERE THE KING AND HIS BROTHER DEFEATED THE VIKING ARMY.

VIKING SHIPS

The Vikings were famous for their shipbuilding skills and were the best sailors of their time. They used their ships for fishing, for carrying *merchandise* that could be traded with other countries and for transporting warriors to new places that were to be invaded.

VIKING LONGSHIPS WERE OFTEN CALLED 'THE SERPENTS OF THE SEA' BECAUSE OF THE CARVINGS IN THE SHAPE OF FIERCE DRAGONS OR SNAKES AT THE PROW (THE FRONT OF THE SHIP).

Viking warships were called longships and they were very fast and sturdy. They were 'clinker-built', meaning that they were made out of wood and were held together with iron rivets (metal pins). They could hold up to 60 men and were powered by oars and a sail.

MANY SHIPS AND BOATS TODAY ARE STILL 'CLINKER-BUILT', USING RIVETS TO HOLD PLANKS OF WOOD TOGETHER.

Longships were mostly built from oakwood, and any gaps between the planks were filled with animal hair and wool to make sure that the ship would not let any water in.

The ships were designed to be narrow and flexible so that the sailors could control them in stormy seas and move them through shallow waters.

The Vikings also built lots of small boats that were used for many different things, including fishing and carrying people across rivers. These were small rowing boats that were either carried aboard the larger ships or towed behind them.

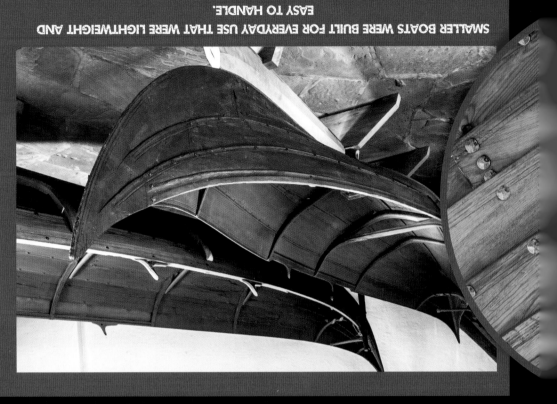

SMALLER BOATS WERE BUILT FOR EVERYDAY USE THAT WERE LIGHTWEIGHT AND EASY TO HANDLE.

The Vikings also built ships to carry *cargo*. These were wider, deeper and slower than the longships. They were called knarrs. These ships had fewer oars as cargo was heavier and more difficult to move through the water than warriors or merchandise. The sailors on knarrs relied more on wind power than the sailors on the longships, so the masts were much longer and the sails were much bigger. These ships were also used to explore distant places, carry livestock and transport people's belongings if they were settling in a new place.

Viking shipbuilders used wool to make sails as it contains a natural oil, called lanolin, that is waterproof.

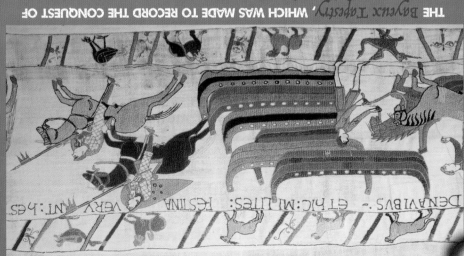

THE *Bayeux Tapestry*, WHICH WAS MADE TO RECORD THE CONQUEST OF ENGLAND BY *William the Conqueror*, SHOWS BOATS SIMILAR TO THOSE USED BY THE VIKINGS.

EVERYDAY LIFE

In their homelands, most Vikings were farmers or fishermen. Many were also craftsmen and *traders*. When they settled in Britain, they built new villages, towns and cities and brought their old way of life with them.

MANY VIKINGS WERE FARMERS. MEAT WOULD BE USED FOR FOOD AND THE SKINS OF ANIMALS WERE USED FOR CLOTHING.

Most houses were built from wood and had walls made of *wattle and daub*. In places where there were only a few trees, houses were built from stone or earth. Roofs were covered in straw or stone and had one hole in each of them that would have been used as chimney.

Houses would have just had one long room with holes in the walls for windows. There would be a fire in the middle of the room that the women used to cook on.

Viking society was divided into different classes. A king ruled each community and below him were jarls (noblemen), then karls (freemen) and finally thralls (slaves).

Family life was very important to the Vikings. The man was the head of the household and boys in the family would help him with his work. Girls often helped their mothers at home.

Viking children did not go to school. They learned language, history, religion, law and practical skills from their parents. Often they would learn from spoken stories and songs. By the age of 15 or 16 Viking children were considered adults and Viking fathers would often find husbands for their daughters.

SOME EXAMPLES OF VIKING POTTERY THAT WOULD HAVE BEEN USED IN THE HOME EVERY DAY.

ALTHOUGH THERE WERE NO BOOKS, SOME CHILDREN LEARNED HOW TO READ RUNES AND HOW TO CARVE MESSAGES USING THE RUNIC ALPHABET.

Although they were fearsome warriors, the Vikings had a series of sayings relating to how best to live everyday life. This included: 'Be a friend to your friend, match gift with gift; meet smiles with smiles ...'

Viking women were allowed to own land had the right to shar their husband's weal On top of this, they were allowed to divo their husbands and a as traders in their ow right. They were als expected to learn to defend themselves and their homes.

↑

VIKING WOMEN WOULD HAVE HAD THEIR OWN TOOL KNIVES SIMILAR TO THIS ONE HAVE BEEN FOUND IN VIKING GRAVES AND ARE CALLED WOMEN'S KNIVES.

The Vikings spoke a language called Old Norse. When they wanted to write things down they used runes. The runic alphabet was called the 'futhark'. It was called this as this was the sound that the first six letters of the alphabet made if you put them together.

ᚠᚢᚦᚨᚱᚲᚷᚹ ᚺᚾᛁᛃᛇᛈᛉᛊ ᛏᛒᛖᛗᛚᛜᛟᛞ

fuþarkgw hnijïpʀs tbemlŋdo

IN OLD NORSE THE WORD RUNE MEANS 'LETTER', 'TEXT' OR 'INSCRIPTION'.

The shape of runic letters meant that they were easy to carve into metal, bone or stone. Because these materials rot very slowly, many carvings still survive today. Sometimes *runestones* were used as signs to mark boundaries or as *memorials*.

The Old Norse language has developed into the modern languages of Danish, Norwegian and Swedish. However, the modern language that is closest to Old Norse is Icelandic.

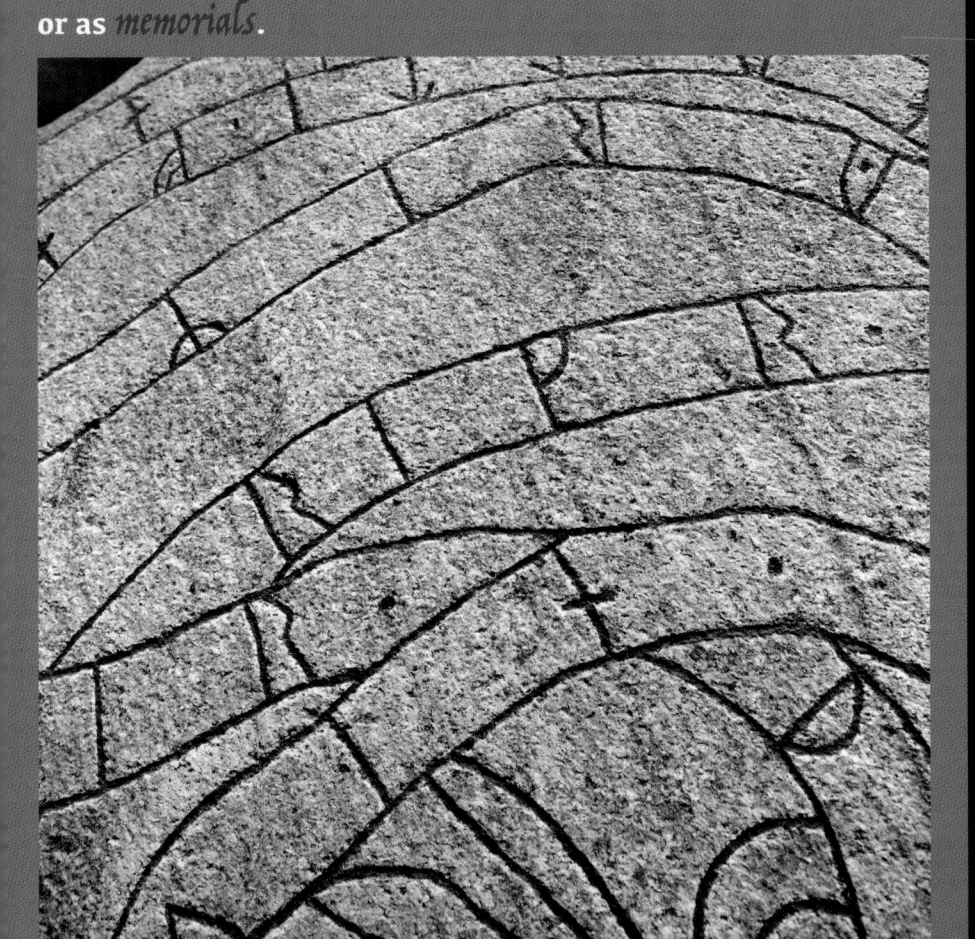

AN EXAMPLE OF AN ANCIENT RUNESTONE, CARVED WITH LETTERS FROM THE FUTHARK.

THE WORD RUNE MEANS 'MYSTERY' OR 'SECRET' AND SOME PEOPLE BELIEVE THAT RUNES CARVED INTO PEBBLES OR WOOD CAN BE USED TO TELL FORTUNES.

The Vikings were great storytellers, but there were no books until late in the Viking Age. They would pass down stories of great heroes, battles and warriors by word of mouth. Some of these ancient stories have become known as sagas.

Towards the end of the Viking Age, some of the sagas were written down. Some, such as Eirik's Saga, are very famous. As well as showing us the importance of storytelling in Viking life, they also give us lots of historical information and detail.

THE VIKING SAGA 'THE CURSE OF ANDVARI'S RING' MAY HAVE GIVEN J.R.R. TOLKIEN THE INSPIRATION TO WRITE 'THE LORD OF THE RINGS'.

THIS PICTURE IS AN ILLUSTRATION FOR THE POEM 'HAUSTLÖNG', WHICH TELLS THE STORY OF THREE GODS.

GRETTIR OVERTHROWS THORIR REDBEAR

GRETTIR THE STRONG WAS A FAMOUS OUTLAW WHO FEATURED IN ONE OF THE VIKINGS' MOST POPULAR SAGAS.

Poetry was popular with kings and noblemen in Viking times. They would often show off to guests by paying poets, known as 'skalds', to recite poems or sing songs about Viking victories, or to praise them and their friends.

Christopher Columbus is famous for discovering America in 1492. But historians believe that Eirik's Saga tells the story of the Vikings finding North America almost 500 years before Columbus did.

CLOTHES AND JEWELLERY

The Vikings often had to deal with cold climates, so they wore many layers of clothing to keep themselves warm. Men would wear an under-shirt and trousers with knee length tunics belted around the waist. Women would wear long under-dresses with pinafores over the top in order to stay warm.

Vikings liked their clothes to look good and would often wear embroidered cloth and heavy metal jewellery to show their position in society.

CLOTH WAS COLOURED USING PLANTS. FOR EXAMPLE LICHEN, WHICH CAN BE FOUND ON TREES AND ROCKS, WAS USED TO MAKE DIFFERENT COLOURS SUCH AS YELLOW, PURPLE AND GREEN.

HERE ARE SOME EXAMPLES OF VIKING CLOTHING. THESE REPLICAS ARE KEPT IN A VIKING MUSEUM IN SWEDEN.

Viking women spun, wove, dyed and sewed to make clothes. They would use materials such as the fibres inside the stems of hemp plants and stinging nettles or the wool from sheep to weave their fabrics. They then used plants to dye them.

Rich Vikings liked their clothes to be bright and colourful, meaning that individual strands of thread were often dyed before they were woven together to make patterned garments. Sometimes gold or silver thread was used to edge their clothes.

Vikings would wear big, strong brooches in order to fasten their capes. These brooches were often very detailed, with intricate patterns and decoration. The brooches worn by rich Vikings were decorated with precious stones.

MEN WOULD WEAR BROOCHES LIKE THIS ONE ON THEIR RIGHT SHOULDERS, WHEREAS WOMEN WOULD WEAR THEM ON EITHER SHOULDER AND WOULD USE THEM TO FASTEN THEIR SHAWLS.

Viking jewellery was very important in Viking society. Vikings wore brooches, rings, bracelets and neck rings to show their social position. The poor would wear jewellery made of animal bones, pewter or bronze. The rich would wear designs of silver and gold with amber, crystals and glass.

THIS BRACELET WAS FOUND BY ARCHAEOLOGISTS IN SILVERDALE, ENGLAND ALONGSIDE HUNDREDS OF OTHER PIECES OF VIKING TREASURE THAT HAD BEEN BURIED THERE.

Viking jewellers were nicknamed 'cinder blowers' because their faces were often blackened by the fires they used to do their work.

Both men and women loved wearing jewellery. They would wear rings, bracelets and necklac... Many pieces featured detailed carvings of animals, especially the twisting heads of serpents.

FOOD AND DRINK

Vikings ate two meals a day, one in the morning and one in the evening. Food was usually simple and involved lots of grains. Most people ate a lot of bread, which was made by mixing barley and rye with water. It went stale very quickly, so women baked new bread daily.

GRAINS, SUCH AS OATS, WHEAT, BARLEY AND RYE, WERE AN IMPORTANT PART OF THE VIKING DIET.

→

The Vikings also ate lots of fish, meat, cheese and milk. They would often grill meat on a stick over a fire or place it onto hot rocks in order to roast it. Sometimes they boiled food in pits lined with wood or animal skin.

Salt and pepper was easily available, but wealthier Vikings would sometimes use spices that were brought over from other countries to flavour their food.

Vikings also ate food that had been *preserved* through drying or salting. These foods were especially good for travelling or in the winter, as other meats and grains weren't available. They would often smear butter on dried fish and meat to make it nicer to eat.

← VIKINGS PRESERVED RAW MEAT OR FISH BY DRYING IT OVER SMOKE, RUBBING IT IN SALT OR PICKLING IT IN SOUR MILK.

Vikings would use clay or metal pots for cooking. Other *utensils*, such as ladles, spoons and knives, were usually made out of wood or metal. Food would be served on a wooden platter and eaten with fingers and knives.

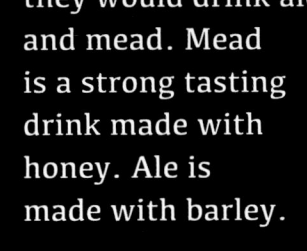

Drinks, such as milk and water, were drank every day. Wine was rare and expensive, so on special occasions they would drink ale and mead. Mead is a strong tasting drink made with honey. Ale is made with barley.

THIS EXAMPLE OF A REPLICA VIKING DRINKING HORN HAS DETAILED DECORATION AROUND THE RIM. ←

Vikings would drink from either wooden cups or drinking horns, which would have been made out of the horn of a cow. Rich people would have them decorated with carvings of silver or gold and would wear them on their belts.

SPORTS, GAMES AND MUSIC

Playing sports was a good way for Viking men and boys to show off their strength, fitness and skill and was often used as training for war. Games included swimming, wrestling, running, jumping, skating and weightlifting.

Other games included a tug-of-war, which was another way of showing off strength. The men were very competitive and their sporting activities would often end in injury. It is believed that wrestling was sometimes used as a kind of duel to settle arguments.

TUG-OF-WAR IS STILL PLAYED ACROSS THE WORLD TODAY. IT IS BELIEVED THAT AS WELL AS SHOWING STRENGTH, THE BACK AND FORTH MOTIONS NEEDED TO PLAY HELPED THE VIKINGS TO IMPROVE THEIR ROWING SKILLS.

Viking men liked to watch violent fights between animals, especially horses. They would make bets on which horse would win the fight.

Viking boys would have spent a lot of time playing war games. Boys and girls played a game called Kingy Bats, which was played with a bat and ball. Children also played with carved dolls and figures.

LITTLE BOYS WOULD PREPARE THEMSELVES FOR FIGHTING WHEN THEY GREW UP BY PLAYING WAR GAMES WITH WOODEN SWORDS.

Vikings also liked to play games in their homes. Carved shapes, like chess pieces, have been discovered, which may have been used for board games. Hneftafl, which means 'the King's table', was a popular board game and involved one player protecting a king from an army.

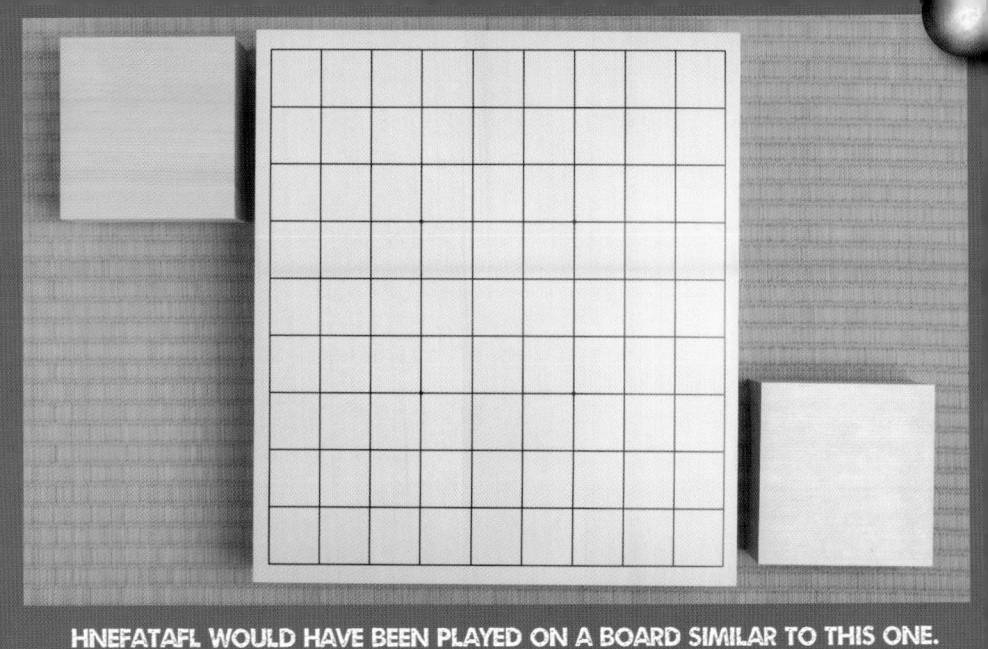

HNEFATAFL WOULD HAVE BEEN PLAYED ON A BOARD SIMILAR TO THIS ONE.

Viking families liked to share stories with each other and recite famous sagas. As well as being entertaining, this was an important way of passing down Viking history from generation to generation.

During Viking times there was no system for writing down music, so there are no records of what Viking music really sounded like.

VIKINGS LIKED TO PLAY MUSIC AND SING. THE DRUMS THEY USED WOULD HAVE LOOKED SIMILAR TO THESE.

Music was important to the Vikings. Songs were played on harps, whistles and drums. Sometimes professional entertainers travelled from village to village reciting poems, playing music and telling stories.

THESE PEOPLE ARE TAKING PART IN A VIKING RE-ENACTMENT DAY, DRESSING UP AS VIKINGS AND PLAYING VIKING MUSIC.

GODS, MYTHS AND LEGENDS

The Vikings worshipped many different gods and goddesses. They believed that the gods would take care of them if they prayed before going into battle or setting off on long journeys. They offered the gods food and drink in return for good luck.

Valkyries were sky-goddesses who flew high above battles. They collected the spirits of men who died bravely in battle and carried them off to Valhalla, which was the name given to warrior heaven.

THIS PICTURE STONE SHOWS AN IMAGE OF A VALKYRIES HELPING WARRIORS ON THEIR WAY TO VALHALLA.

Odin was the god of war. The Vikings believed that he was wise and could see into the future. Thor, the god of thunder who ruled over the weather, was believed to be very strong. Frey and his sister Freya were generous and life-giving.

Vikings would pray in wooden temples and offer animals to the gods as sacrifices.

THIS IS AN ILLUSTRATION OF THOR, THE GOD OF THUNDER. THE VIKINGS BELIEVED HE CARRIED A HUGE HAMMER.

Viking men and women believed in elves, giants, trolls and other spirits. They loved stories about gods, adventurers, monsters and heroes. They liked to carry amulets (charms) to protect themselves. Many were shaped like the magical hammer Thor used to fight giants and monsters.

AMULETS LIKE THIS ONE WERE WORN AS LUCKY CHARMS FOR PROTECTION. PEOPLE TODAY STILL WEAR LUCKY CHARMS. →

Myths and legends were passed down through word of mouth. As well as stories about the gods, there were many magical and fantastical stories that took place in a world inhabited by humans, which the Vikings called Midgard. The gods and goddesses lived in Asgard and the two places were believed to be linked by a bridge known as Bifröst.

Viking myths and legends are still popular as stories today, with hundreds of books featuring the gods, monsters and trolls that the Vikings believed in.

VIKING MYTHS AND LEGENDS WEREN'T WRITTEN DOWN BY THE VIKINGS THEMSELVES, BUT WERE WRITTEN DOWN LATER IN MANUSCRIPTS LIKE THIS ONE, WHICH TELLS THE STORY OF ODIN.

THIS IMAGE SHOWS A GOD BEING BROUGHT BACK TO ASGARD, AS TOLD IN ONE OF THE MANY MYTHS AND LEGENDS OF THE VIKINGS.

Stories of Viking gods, myths and legends were passed on by word of mouth through families and friends. They were only written down much later on. These stories help us to understand Viking beliefs and their history.

VIKING BURIALS

Vikings believed in life after death, so dead people were often buried with their belongings so that they could take their things with them into the next world. The graves of ordinary people were often marked by stones laid out in the shape of a ship.

↓ BENEATH THIS VIKING BURIAL MOUND IN ARDNUMURCHAN, SCOTLAND LIES THE FIRST VIKING BURIAL SHIP TO BE FOUND STILL IN ONE PIECE ON MAINLAND BRITAIN. IT IS 1,000 YEARS OLD.

THIS IS A VIKING BURIAL SITE MARKED BY STONES IN THE SHAPE OF A SHIP. ↑

The bodies and belongings of rich and important Vikings, such as Viking kings, chiefs and noblemen, were placed inside ships. The ships were then buried and covered by a mound of earth. It is possible to see burial mounds like this all around the world.

Vikings believed that the dead had to make a long journey to the *afterlife* after they died. Because of this, Vikings would often be buried with their horses and carts so that they were prepared for the journey.

Vikings would also be buried with food in order to help them on their journey to the afterlife.

THIS ARTIST'S DRAWING SHOWS HOW THE VIKING SHIP AT ARDNAMURCHAN WOULD HAVE LOOKED WHEN IT WAS BURIED. ↑

Some Vikings' bodies were burned after death. As they burned, relatives would bend their weapons and any armour in the hot ash. Some important Vikings were burned in ships to show special respect. The flaming ship would be launched into the sea.

THIS PAINTING SHOWS A VIKING SHIP BEING SET ALIGHT AND PUSHED INTO THE SEA.

Towards the end of the Viking Age, Vikings in Britain started to use carved gravestones to mark the site of a burial. These often featured carvings of animals that were painted in bright colours. Vikings would wait for seven days after a funeral to hold the *wake*.

Sometimes when rich Vikings died, their slaves would be killed and buried alongside them.

Many traditional Viking burial ceremonies began to disappear when Christianity spread through the Scandinavian invaders. The Viking settlers in England were the first to give up their own religion.

THIS VIKING GRAVESTONE IS CALLED A HOGBACK STONE BECAUSE OF ITS CURVED SHAPE. IT WAS FOUND IN A CHURCHYARD IN SCOTLAND.

When the Vikings invaded Britain, they brought with them many new skills and traditions that can still be seen in Britain today. The Viking *legacy* lives on in landscapes and people all over the world.

WOODEN BOAT BUILDERS THROUGHOUT THE WORLD CONTINUE TO MAKE CLINKER-BUILT BOATS THAT GLIDE THROUGH THE WATER USING OARS, SAILS OR MOTORS. SOME BOATBUILDING SCHOOLS TEACH STUDENTS TO BUILD BOATS LIKE THE VIKINGS DID.

THE VIKINGS USED ICE SKATES MADE OUT OF BONES TO HELP THEM MOVE ACROSS THE LAND IN THEIR HOME COUNTRIES. ICE SKATES LOOK VERY DIFFERENT NOW, THEY ARE MUCH STRONGER AND USED FOR SPORT INSTEAD OF WORK OR AS A MEANS OF TRANSPORT.

THE VIKINGS WERE EXCELLENT CRAFTSMEN, AND MADE LEATHER, WEAPONS, CLOTHES AND JEWELLERY. VIKING STYLE JEWELLERY IS STILL VERY POPULAR TODAY AND PEOPLE OFTEN WEAR BANGLES, RINGS AND NECKLACES FEATURING ENGRAVINGS SIMILAR TO THOSE USED BY THE VIKINGS. →

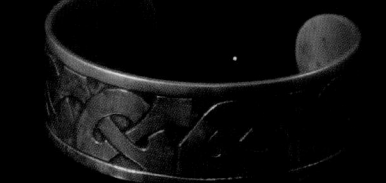

Vikings were feared across Europe and as they spread, smaller countries began to work together in order to become stronger. Through history, smaller countries continued to do this so that they were better able to defend themselves.

When the Vikings invaded and settled in a country, they often married local women and had families. Many people in Britain are *descended* from Vikings and it is thought that up to fifty percent of people in the north and south-east of the country might have a Viking ancestor.

WE STILL USE MANY VIKING WORDS IN THE ENGLISH LANGUAGE TODAY. THE WORDS EGG, ROOT, SISTER, HUSBAND AND KID ALL COME FROM OLD NORSE, WHICH IS THE LANGUAGE OF THE VIKINGS. THURSDAY GETS ITS NAME FROM THE GOD THOR. WEDNESDAY COMES FROM ODIN, WHO WAS SOMETIMES CALLED WODEN.

THE VIKINGS WERE AHEAD OF THEIR TIME IN RECOGNISING WOMEN'S RIGHTS. VIKING WOMEN WERE CONSIDERED TO BE VERY IMPORTANT FOR RUNNING FARMS AND WERE ABLE TO DIVORCE THEIR HUSBANDS WHILE KEEPING PART OF THEIR WEALTH.

Viking criminal trials took place at a 'ting'. A group of 12 men, called a jury, would decide whether or not the accused was guilty. Trial by jury is now common in many countries around the world.

Many Viking place names are still used today. Place names ending in –dale (valley), –kirk (church) and –beck (stream) can be found all over Britain. Places ending in –by, such as Derby, used to be Viking farms or villages.

TIMELINE

AD 789

The first ever recorded attack by the Vikings takes place at Portland in Dorset.

AD 793

Vikings attack the monastery at Lindisfarne on the north-east coast of England.

AD 795

Vikings attack the monastery on Iona, a Scottish island.

AD 867

The Viking army kills rival kings in Northumbria and conquers Jorvik (York).

AD 869

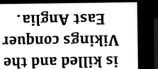

Edmund, the King of the East Angles, is killed and the Vikings conquer East Anglia.

AD 870

The Vikings destroy Dumbarton in northern Britain.

AD 871

Ethelred and Alfred of Wessex battle with the Vikings. Ethelred is killed, and Alfred becomes King.

AD 874

The Vikings conquer the kingdom of Mercia.

Timeline

AD 878 — Wessex is overrun by Vikings and Alfred goes into hiding.

AD 886 — Alfred of Wessex dies and his son, Edward the Elder, takes over. At this time, Wessex was the only kingdom in England not taken by the Vikings.

AD 954 — Eric Bloodaxe, the last Viking King of England, is forced out of Jorvik (York).

AD 1042 — Edward the Confessor becomes King of England.

AD 877 — Welsh king Rhodri Mawr is defeated by the Vikings.

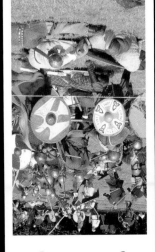

AD 886 — Alfred, king of Wessex, agrees to share England with the Vikings.

AD 937 — Athelstan of Wessex destroys Viking and Scottish armies at Brunanbuh.

AD 1016 — King Canute of Denmark becomes King of England.

AD 1066 — Edward the Confessor dies and is succeeded by Harold, Earl of Wessex. The Battle of Hastings took place and the Norman conquest of England began.

QUICK QUIZ

1. Where did the Vikings come from?

2. What year did the Vikings attack Lindisfarne?

3. What was the most powerful kingdom in England before the Vikings invaded?

4. What was the name of the city in Northumbria that the Vikings invaded?

5. In what year was the Battle of Ashdown?

6. What does 'clinker-built' mean?

7. What are 'knarrs'?

8. What were most Viking houses built out of?

9. What is the runic alphabet called?

10. What are 'skalds'?

11. What did Vikings use to fasten their capes?

12. What nickname was given to Viking jewellers?

13. How many meals a day did Vikings eat?

14. What are 'Kingy Bats'?

15. Who was the Viking God of thunder?

16. What is a Valkyrie?

17. What is a burial mound?

18. What did Vikings have buried with them when they died?

19. Can you think of three words that we use today that are Viking words?

20. What did Vikings use to dye fabrics?

memorials	items that are made to remember a person, place or event
merchandise	goods for sale
merchants	people who sell goods
plunder	to steal
replica	an exact copy or model of something
runes	letters in the Viking alphabet
runestones	small stones with the Viking alphabet carved into them
settlements	places where people choose to live and build communities
society	lots of people living together in a collection of communities
traders	people who trade in goods
utensils	tools
Viking Age	the era in history when Vikings were most prominent
wake	a gathering either before or after a funeral
wattle and daub	a way of building walls using sticks and mud
William the Conqueror	King of England from 1066 to 1087

INDEX